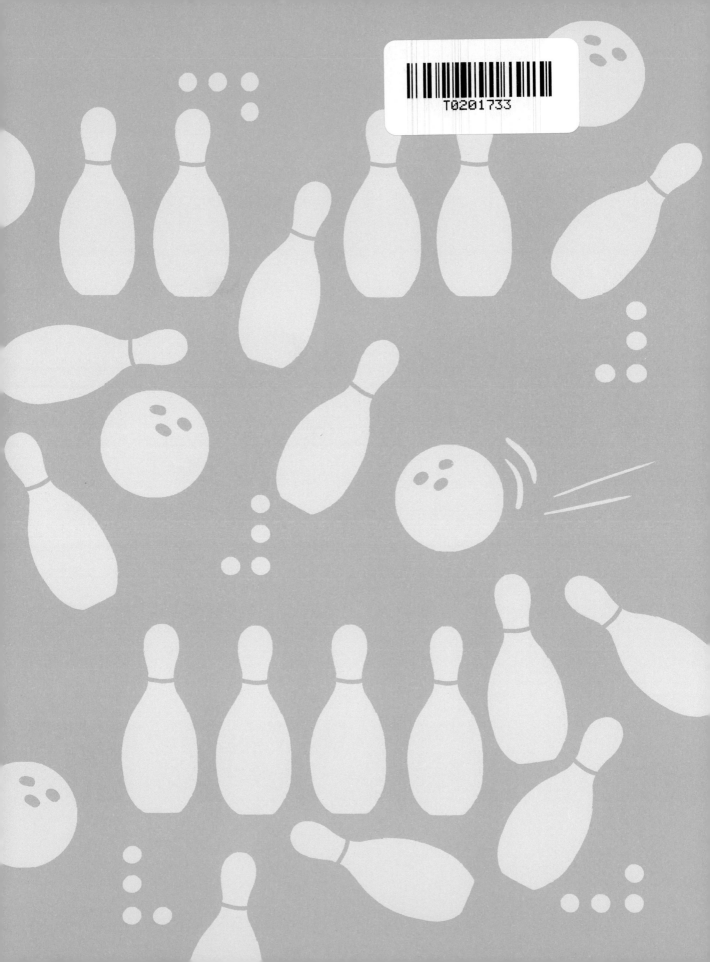

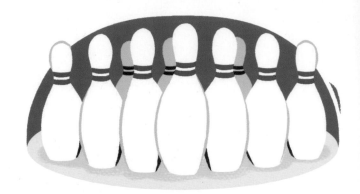

For Lina & Waiyen x
—SGC

Sital Gorasia Chapman is passionate about bringing math to life for kids. She worked in finance before becoming a children's author.

Consultant Steph King works with educators to improve math teaching and learning in the classroom. She has written many math books for children.

DK | Penguin Random House

Author Sital Gorasia Chapman
Mathematics Advisor Steph King
Illustrator Susanna Rumiz

Editors Laura Gilbert, Rea Pikula
Senior Designer Rachael Parfitt
US Senior Editor Shannon Beatty
Senior Production Editor Nikoleta Parasaki
Senior Production Controller Ben Radley
Jacket Coordinator Elin Woosnam
Managing Editor Penny Smith
Art Director Mabel Chan
Publisher Francesca Young
Managing Director Sarah Larter

First American Edition, 2024
Published in the United States by DK Publishing,
a division of Penguin Random House LLC
1745 Broadway, 20th Floor, New York, NY 10019

Text copyright © 2024 Sital Gorasia Chapman
Artwork and design copyright © 2024 Dorling
Kindersley Limited

24 25 26 27 28 10 9 8 7 6 5 4 3 2 1
001–332644–Oct/2024

Published in Great Britain by Dorling Kindersley Limited

A catalog record for this book
is available from the Library of Congress.
ISBN 978-0-5938-4363-5

DK books are available at special discounts when purchased in bulk for sales promotions, premiums, fund-raising, or educational use.
For details, contact: DK Publishing Special Markets,
1745 Broadway, 20th Floor, New York, NY 10019
SpecialSales@dk.com

Printed and bound in China

www.dk.com

The Math Adventurers

Go Bowling

DK

Beep and Boots invited
several good friends to compete
in a bowling competition,
with a prize so super sweet.

The group of 12 divided
in two equal teams to play.
But six was just too many.
They got in each other's way.

The halves were split in half again
to make four teams of three.
But still this wouldn't work
since there were only three lanes free.

Fractions represent equal parts of
a whole. The whole can be a shape or object,
a number, a group (for example,
a group of 6 people) or a measure
(for example, 2 inches).

"We'll have to split up into thirds,"
Beep finally decided.
And into three teams of four
the friends were soon divided.

 When a whole is divided into two equal parts, each part is called a half and can be written as ½.

 When a whole is divided into four equal parts, each part is called a quarter and can be written as ¼. A quarter is half of a half.

 When a whole is divided into three equal parts, each part is called a third and can be written as ⅓.

Beep headed up team one.
10 pins were in her sight.
She swung her arm behind her
and let the ball take flight.

She watched it quickly spinning
down the middle of the lane.
Then...

...swerve into the gutter.
Oh no! What a shame!

She did a little better
with her second bowling ball.
The left pin wobbled wildly,
but still it did not fall.

Boots was the commander
of the players in team two.
She picked the biggest bowling ball...

Up next was team number three,
led by little Joe.
Half the pins were toppled
on his very first go.

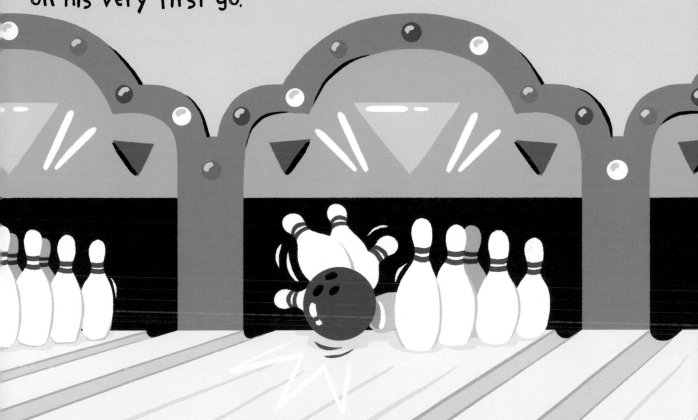

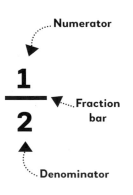

A fraction has two parts.
The denominator is below the line
and tells us how many equal parts
there are in the whole.
The numerator is above the line
and tells us how many of these
equal parts we are counting.
(And the line is called a
fraction bar.)

Numerator

$\dfrac{1}{2}$

Fraction
bar

Denominator

Beep cheered on her teammates while she waited for her turn, and spilled half her apple juice into the ball return!

Fractions have a place on a number line.

One half (½) is exactly halfway between 0 and 1.

²⁄₄ is the same as ½.

Player after player
took their turn to bowl.
The championship trophy
was each team's final goal.

Beep lined up another ball
and carefully took aim.
It still missed every single pin.
"I don't like this game!"

Beep tried aiming to the left,
and tried aiming to the right.

She tried standing super tall,
and crouched down to half her height.

But no matter how she bowled it,
no matter what she tried,
the pins were all still standing,
while the ball rolled down the side.

Her teammates tried consoling her,
but Beep had had enough.
"I'm not playing anymore!"
She sat down in a huff.

She crossed her arms in front of her,
looked down, and turned away.
While the other players carried on,
half the game was still to play.

But when Boots flattened all 10 pins,
Beep jumped up from her chair.
She clapped and cheered and hugged her friend,
then twirled her in the air.

"I guess it doesn't matter
if I hit the whole group, half, or none.
It matters that we play together
and we all have fun."

	1	2	3	4	5	6	7	8	9
Beep's Bowlers	– –	1 /	5 /	4 5	– –	1 /	9 /	2 /	3 6
	0	15	29	38	38	57	69	82	91
Boots & Friends	– –	3 /	– 8	1 7	6 /	9 /	9 –	X	3 1
	0	10	18	26	45	64	73	87	91
Joe's Team	5 –	2 7	7 /	1 7	4 /	2 7	6 /	8 /	2 7
	5	14	25	33	45	54	72	84	93

The scores before the final round
showed Joe's team in the lead.
Beep and Boots, neck and neck,
worked out the points they'd need.

Beep put down a bowling ball
and rolled with all her strength.
It traveled super slowly down
lane number two's full length.

It bumped into the front pin and made a mighty clatter. She looked on in amazement as the pins began to scatter.

Six tenths of the pins went down,
four tenths were left to fall.
Could she get the other four?
Could she get them all?

Three quarters of the standing pins
were knocked down to the ground.
Beep did a celebration dance,
high-fived her friends all around.

10 rounds complete, the game was done.
The final scores were in.
100 points went to each team.
It was a three-way win!

The prize was shared between the players,
one twelfth for each one.
Beep said, "When can we play again?
Bowling's super fun!"

A whole can be divided equally into
two halves, three thirds, four
quarters, five fifths, six sixths,
seven sevenths, and so on.

GLOSSARY

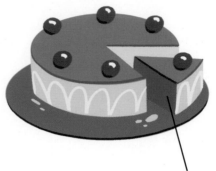

Whole – a complete shape, object, group, or number

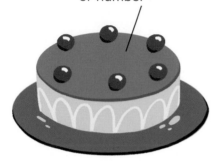

Fraction – a fraction represents equal parts of a whole

Half (½) – one part of something that has been equally divided in two

Third (⅓) – one part of something that has been equally divided in three

Quarter (¼) – half of a half; one part of something that has been equally divided in four

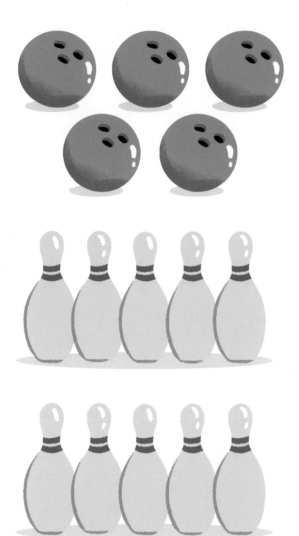

Fifth (⅕) – one part of something that has been equally divided in five

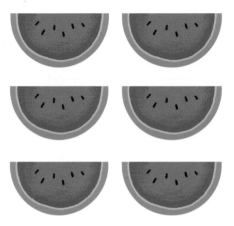

Sixth (⅙) – one part of something that has been equally divided in six

Tenth (¹⁄₁₀) – one part of something that has been equally divided in ten

Numerator – the number of equal parts we are counting

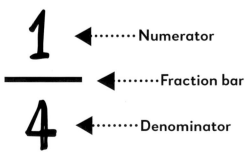

1 ◀······ **Numerator**

─── ◀······ **Fraction bar**

4 ◀······ **Denominator**

Denominator – the number of equal parts in the whole

QUESTIONS

1. What is ¼ of 8?

2. What is a quarter of 12?

3. What is ¾ of 12?

4. Beep has 4 quarters of an apple. How many quarters would be equal to half of an apple?

5. If three friends share a pie equally, what fraction of the pie do they each get?

6. How many quarters in a whole?

7. Boots has some grapes. She gives half of them to Beep. Boots has 5 grapes left. How many grapes did she have to start with?

8. Which of these shapes does not show halves?

A   C

B   D

9. A train journey takes half an hour. A bus journey takes a quarter of an hour longer. How long is the bus journey?

10. What fraction of this pizza has mushrooms?

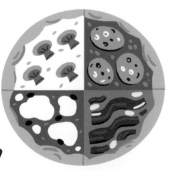

ANSWERS

1. 2
2. 3
3. 9
4. 2 quarters
5. One third (⅓)
6. 4
7. 10 grapes
8. C
9. Three quarters of an hour
10. One quarter (¼)

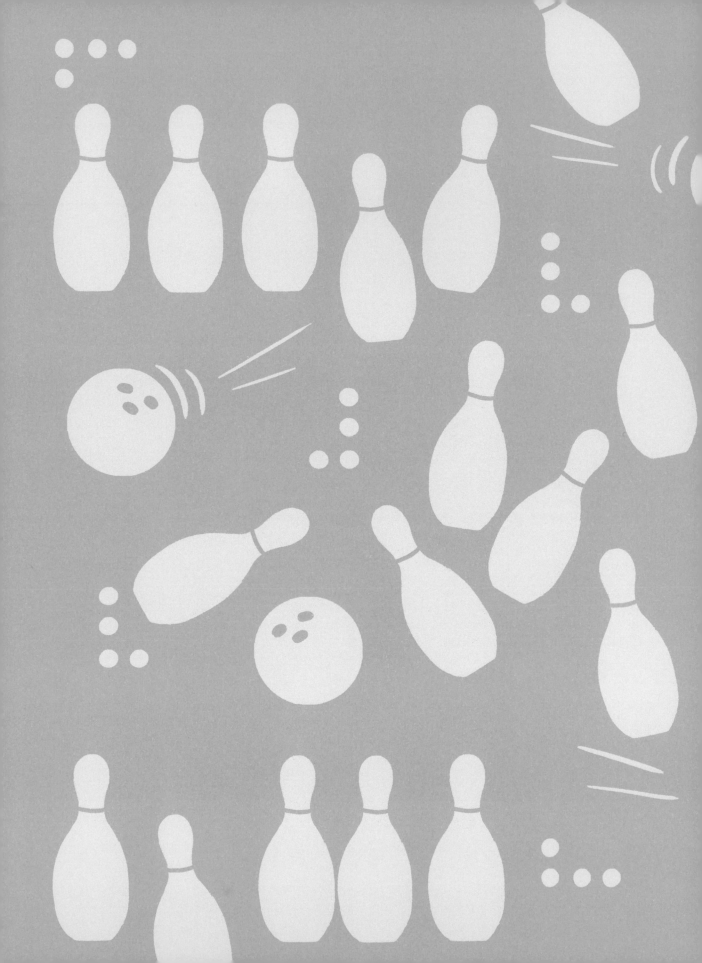